'This book is for any adult seeking some kind of template for communicating with a child who, through no fault of their own, is having to cope with a number of obstacles ... Problems can be overcome Mine's book tells us: with kindness, listening and talisman-like keepers that remind us to be kind, talk to each other and to have empathy.'

Sir Lenny Henry, *CBE*

'A much-needed resource to support parents, caregivers and other adults around a child experiencing adversity. Often, adults have a fear of speaking to a child about their experiences, not knowing what to say, or how to be, or whether they might make the situation worse. The storybook and its guide scaffold and hold the adult safely, helping a child to reflect on their own thoughts and feelings while in the safety of story. Exploring the emotions and feelings of Maya with a trusted adult will undoubtedly help the child to make sense of their own experiences. What is shareable is bearable!'

Julie Harmieson, *Trauma-Informed Schools UK (TISUK)*
Director of Education and National Strategy

Nurturing Children's Resilience Following Adverse Childhood Experiences

Alongside the accompanying storybook, *Maya's ACE Adventures!*, this guide provides adults with much-needed resources to talk with children about their traumatic experiences in ways that are non-threatening, safe and can build a child's confidence in speaking about their fears with a trusted adult.

Designed to be read by an adult *before* they read the story together with a child, this guide provides practical tools, such as scene-by-scene discussion prompts and strategies for co-regulation (CR), to facilitate conversations that are informed, relaxed and allow for healing from grief and trauma. These tools are contextualised by a detailed examination and critique of the adverse childhood experiences (ACEs) framework, in addition to an overview of the neurobiology involved in the stress response, to support adults and alleviate their anxiety about asking the right questions and having the right answers for the children they support.

Together with the storybook, this guide is essential reading for teachers, parents, foster carers, social workers and other professionals who are supporting children, by giving them the resources they need to foster hope and resilience among children who have survived traumatic experiences.

Dr Mine Conkbayir is an award-winning author, trainer and researcher passionate about bridging the knowledge gap between neuroscience and the early years (EY) sector. A key contributor to the Birth to Five Matters non-statutory guidance for the Early Years Foundation Stage and designer of the first-ever neuroscience-informed qualifications for the EY sector, her award-winning book, *Early Childhood and Neuroscience. Theory, Research and Implications for Practice*, is in its second edition and her latest book, *The Neuroscience of the Developing Child. Self-Regulation for Wellbeing and a Sustainable Future* is out now.

Nurturing Children's Resilience Following Adverse Childhood Experiences

An Adult Guide

Written by Dr Mine Conkbayir

Illustrated by Chloe Evans

Routledge
Taylor & Francis Group

LONDON AND NEW YORK

Designed cover image: Artwork by Chloe Evans

First published 2024
by Routledge
4 Park Square, Milton Park, Abingdon, Oxon OX14 4RN

and by Routledge
605 Third Avenue, New York, NY 10158

Routledge is an imprint of the Taylor & Francis Group, an informa business

British Library Cataloguing-in-Publication Data
A catalogue record for this book is available from the British Library

Library of Congress Cataloging-in-Publication Data
Names: Conkbayir, Mine, author.
Title: Nurturing children's resilience following adverse childhood experiences :
    an adult guide / Written by Mine Conkbayir ; Illustrated by Chloe Evans.
Description: Abingdon, Oxon ; New York, NY : Routledge, 2023.
Identifiers: LCCN 2022061047 (print) | LCCN 2022061048 (ebook) |
    ISBN 9781032368184 (pbk) | ISBN 9781032367934 (set) |
    ISBN 9781003333920 (ebk)
Subjects: LCSH: Child psychology. | Resilience (Personality trait) in children.
Classification: LCC BF721 .C595 2023 (print) | LCC BF721 (ebook) |
    DDC 155.4—dc23/eng/20230415
LC record available at https://lccn.loc.gov/2022061047
LC ebook record available at https://lccn.loc.gov/2022061048

ISBN: 978-1-032-36818-4 (pbk)
ISBN: 978-1-003-33392-0 (ebk)

DOI: 10.4324/b23180

Typeset in Din
by Apex CoVantage, LLC

This Book is Dedicated to

The storybook, *Maya's ACE Adventures!* and this adult guide are dedicated to all children who have had to overcome many struggles through no fault of their own.

To every one of those children, I say – **you** are a very special and valuable person. You are strong and – you can be whatever you wish to be.

Never let anyone make you think any different.

Lots of love, from Mine.

Contents

Contents

Figures and Tables

Figures

Tables

Introduction

This adult guide is designed to accompany the storybook, *Maya's ACE Adventures! A Story to Celebrate Children's Resilience Following Adverse Childhood Experiences.*

The story of resilience and hope and this accompanying guide are designed to equip the adult to support the emotional wellbeing of children who have been exposed to ACEs.

Read on to find out about some of the key features of this guide, who it is designed for and how it should be used, to ensure that the child reaps the benefits, while being protected from any psychological harm.

> Before you continue, it cannot be emphasized enough that the story and this guide must only be read in the context of a safe relationship – one in which the child feels secure and comfortable with the adult.
>
> Before you read the storybook with the child, read this guide carefully, giving yourself plenty of time to familiarize yourself with the discussion prompts and questions, so that when you do read the book together, your conversation is informed but relaxed and enjoyable. You must avoid making the experience stressful, nor should you ask any leading questions to the child, because this might distress them while compromising an investigation that might already be underway.

Speaking *with* children who have been affected by traumatic experiences plays a critical part in enabling a process of healing and recovery, yet this is still not being done as standard. Research (Baker, et al., 2019; Callaghan, et al., 2015; Allnock and Miller, 2013) continues to demonstrate that children's attempts to disclose abuse and neglect too frequently go unrecognized, unheard or ignored. Your role as a sensitive, active listener is critical and this includes being able to read and accurately interpret the child's non-verbal communication (such as their facial expressions and body language) during your conversation. This is highlighted under Section 31(10) of the Children Act 1989:

> It is important always to take account of the child's reactions, and his or her perceptions, according to the child's age and understanding.
>
> (Voice of the Child, 2022)

When done sensitively and consistently, you can provide children with the necessary support and reassurance to help them express and manage their fears, guide them through their grief and help them recover in a healthy way.

Adults might understandably feel anxious about how to broach the subject, asking the right questions and even having the right answers to any questions that children ask them. This guide is an effective resource for talking with children about the traumatic experiences they have survived in ways that are non-threatening, safe and supportive. When used with the storybook, it can help to build children's confidence in speaking about their experiences with a trusted adult, while ultimately building their resilience.

Key Features of This Guide Include:

- ✔ Information concerning ACEs and their impact across the life trajectory
- ✔ An examination and critique of the ACEs framework
- ✔ An overview of the neurobiology of the stress response
- ✔ CR approaches and strategies to use with the child
- ✔ Scene-by-scene discussion prompts to accompany the story
- ✔ A comprehensive list of resources, helplines and Bibliography, where the reader can find out further information concerning the issues explored in the storybook and guide.

Who This Guide Is Designed For

This guide is written accessibly, in user-friendly language, to encourage use by families, parents, primary carers and foster carers, as well as diverse professionals, including teachers, mentors, social care workers, therapists, counsellors, designated safeguarding leads (DSLs) and other professionals, as relevant.

This guide provides a structure for the adult to confidently support a child who has been exposed to ACEs, in ways that are non-pressurizing and appropriate to the child's stage of understanding, while instilling positivity and hope in the process. As identified by Heckman and Karapakula (2019: 16):

> Positive home environments matter more than neighbourhood for adult outcomes.

It is therefore important to equip parents and practitioners alike, to speak directly *with* children (as opposed to *about* them), following exposure to traumatic experiences (Callaghan et al., 2015) – and give them the strategies to overcome these and live a fulfilled life, in which they are able to form healthy, meaningful and mutually supportive relationships. The storybook and this guide provide a necessary vehicle for adults to speak with children who have been affected by ACEs, with a view to empowering them to overcome these traumatic experiences.

Clearly, the story and this guide are not intended to replace the necessary support and interventions provided by social services, the school and the police – they are designed to complement the wraparound support that should already be in place.

DOI: 10.4324/b23180-2

Structure of the Guide

This guide is broadly divided into two parts. The first half focuses on what ACEs are, their relevance to professionals and primary carers alike and their pervasive impact on holistic wellbeing. This is followed by a critique of the ACEs framework – which is important for us all to reflect on, in terms of how we view children affected by ACEs.

The second half of the guide is more practical in nature, with an exploration of the brain and the neurobiology underlying stress behaviours and consequent ability to learn. Some of these behaviours are linked to Maya's behaviours throughout the story, to help give them context. This includes:

- Impaired cognitive processing, including difficulty paying attention, following instructions, focusing on tasks and problem-solving – which all make it more difficult to learn

- Difficulty in self-regulating – this typically looks like heightened sensitivity to stress and difficulty in persisting in the face of challenges

- Low self-efficacy and feelings of helplessness

- Anxiety, depression, social isolation and low self-image.

Self-regulation (SR) is looked at closely, alongside many practical strategies to support the development of children's SR skills – with discussion on why this is critical to do.

Practical guidance is also included concerning how to respond in the case of a child making an in-the-moment disclosure while sharing the story. This is followed by some helpful tips when using the prompts and questions to encourage the child to express their thoughts and feelings – which then leads into the detailed scene-by-scene prompts. The adult is encouraged to refer to these before sharing the story with the child, as well as during the story, if appropriate.

The list of resources and Bibliography at the end of this guide provide further information and guidance on the topics explored.

DOI: 10.4324/b23180-3

Meet the Characters

Familiarizing yourself with the main characters in the story will help you to understand their personalities, thoughts, feelings and intentions – and their roles in the story. This, in turn, will help you to ask children questions based on the characters and events in the story, in line with their lived experiences.

Maya

Maya is a young girl who lives with her mum and her mum's boyfriend. She tends to be quiet but assertive and generally, she enjoys going to school, but sometimes she feels anxious about going. Maya loves learning about space, playing football, drawing and spending time with her pet hamster, Harry and her best friend, Archie.

Maya

Throughout the story, we see Maya exposed to three ACEs – each of which, with support, she manages and even overcomes. These being:

- Her mum frequently arguing with her boyfriend, which results in Maya feeling too anxious to leave her room or go to school

- Her dad being in prison. This gives rise to mixed emotions in Maya

- Maya being picked on at school, due to her dad being in prison.

As mentioned, Maya is able to overcome these ACEs because of the various types of support in her life. These are also known as protective factors, counter-ACEs or buffers and you will see lots of these throughout the story. By the end of the story, Maya realizes that she *is* resilient and that she *is* able to overcome the difficult events in her life with the help of these protective factors.

DOI: 10.4324/b23180-4

Harry – Maya's Hamster

Harry is one of Maya's best friends. With his silky black coat and huge tuft of golden hair, he never fails to cheer Maya up – even when things get really tough for Maya. He is an outgoing and confident hamster, who loves being with Maya because she cares for him so beautifully. Harry always finds himself in Maya's fantastical journeys in her dreams, where, together, they discover the answer to overcoming Maya's problems in real life.

Maya's Hamster

Archie – Maya's Best Friend

Maya's other best friend is Archie and lucky for her, they are in the same class at school. Archie enjoys going to school and enjoys maths lessons as he loves to solve problems, but most of all, he loves play times, because he can talk to and play with Maya without being told off by the teachers! He has a great sense of humour and can always be relied upon to start off whacky greetings that only he and Maya are allowed to – and manage to do – which we see a glimpse of in the story! Archie is protective of Maya and worries about her wellbeing – which we see when she is picked on by another child at school. He is a loyal friend to Maya.

Archie – Maya's Best Friend

Maya's Mum

Maya's mum is a very kind and gentle person, who does her best to raise Maya. She is separated from Maya's dad – who is serving a prison sentence. Maya's mum and her boyfriend, Deniz, argue frequently and this leaves Maya feeling frightened and upset. Maya's mum often finds herself apologising to Maya about the arguments, as she feels very guilty about Maya witnessing it all. She is very understanding of Maya's mixed feelings about her dad being in prison and always offers simple ways to help overcome her feelings of anger and resentment towards him.

Maya's Mum

Overview of the Story, Maya's ACE Adventures!

The story follows the life of the main character, Maya, who during her childhood is exposed to ACEs. These are extremely harmful experiences which are proven to negatively impact a child's holistic wellbeing and development, particularly if a child is not given consistent support. Exposure to ACEs shapes a child's thoughts, feelings and behaviour on a daily basis. Throughout the story, we see Maya exposed to – and overcome – three ACEs: her dad serving a prison sentence; her mum and her boyfriend frequently arguing (with Maya fearing for her mum's safety) and being picked on at school because of her dad being in prison. But there are lots of protective factors in her life, which are evident all throughout the story. Every night before she goes to sleep, feeling ill at ease, Maya always whispers *"Dreams come tonight, help make it right!"* She and her hamster go on fantastical journeys, where she finds the strength to overcome the problems parallel to her real-life problems. Each time Maya overcomes these problems in her dreams, she is given a *keeper* – a special object to remind her that she is strong and can achieve whatever she wants to. You will notice that with every *keeper* Maya receives, the glow emanating from within her increases – symbolising her increasing resilience. By the end of the story, Maya reflects on all the protective factors in her life and realizes that she is indeed resilient and *can* overcome the more negative aspects of her life.

"When things go wrong, I can be strong!"

DOI: 10.4324/b23180-5

We will now turn our attention to the three main types of stress and ACEs, in order to ensure that you understand what these are and the impact of ACEs on psychological and physical health – across the life trajectory. We will then focus on the storybook, as well as take a whistle-stop tour of the neurobiology of stress behaviours and how you can help children to build their capacity to self-regulate through CR and why this is critical to do.

Stress – Is It All Bad?

Before we look at ACEs specifically, it is first useful to understand that there are three types of stress. Not all types of stress are "bad" – stress is necessary to our survival. That said, some stress is harmful to our wellbeing and ACEs are considered to be one of these three types of stress. It is important to distinguish between these types of stress and the child's stress response to each, so that we are able to respond accordingly. The better you can equip every child to overcome feelings of stress and its impact on the brain and body, the more effectively they can learn how to *identify* and *reduce* the impact of these stressors that have been causing them to feel (for example) frustrated or find it difficult to concentrate. The image, **The Three Types of Stress**, below, outlines the three types of stress and just some of their effects on the child.

The Three Types of Stress

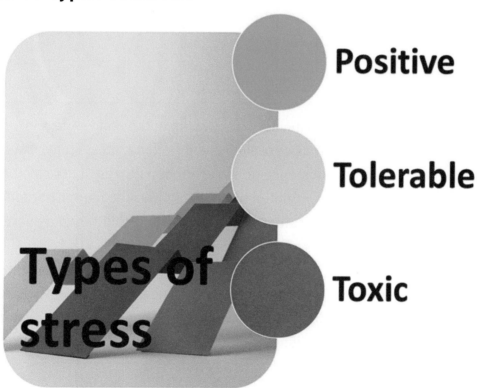

The Three Types of Stress

DOI: 10.4324/b23180-6

Let us now look at some examples for each type of stress.

Positive stress (also known as good stress or eustress) is the most common type of stress. It induces feelings of excitement, anticipation, meaning and happiness. It includes events like a child's first day at school, learning how to ride a bike, taking part in a competition, having a birthday party, or a young adult attending a college interview, meeting a deadline or starting a new job. Once the stressor has been encountered and is over, stress levels (including the key stress hormone, cortisol) return to their normal baseline.

Tolerable stress includes serious but short-term stress like divorce, moving home, the death of a loved one, being involved in a frightening accident, serious illness, injury, worrying about schoolwork or grades, problems with friends, bullying or peer group pressures. Where supportive relationships and networks exist, these types of stress can be overcome with timely and sensitive support, without causing significant, long-term damage to the brain's developing architecture.

Toxic stress can be an isolated incident or ongoing in the child's life and primarily includes ACEs such as sexual abuse, emotional abuse, physical abuse, chronic neglect, caregiver substance abuse or mental illness. It also includes exposure to violence, the accumulated burdens of family economic hardship, living in chaotic or unstable circumstances, like placing children in a succession of foster homes, or displacement due to economic instability, war or a natural disaster – without adequate adult support to enable the child to surmount these ACEs. This commonly results in sustained, heightened activation of the stress response system, which over time, compromises the child's immune system, as well as their mental health, holistic wellbeing, behaviour and ability to learn.

The following chapters provide further information about ACEs (some of which Maya, the main character of the story, is exposed to).

In these chapters you will read about the 10 ACEs as identified in the original ground-breaking study, along with an exploration of how ACEs and trauma interfere with the stress response, behaviour, attention and learning. The potential long-term impact of ACEs on health and wellbeing, as well as those all-important protective factors, are also discussed.

While reading, remember to continually reflect on the information in relation to the children who you read the story with.

ACEs – An Overview

The storybook, *Maya's ACE Adventures!*, is about one young child's exposure to ACEs. What does this term actually mean and why is it relevant to everyone?

ACEs are traumatic events, that are uncontrollable to the child, occurring from in utero, which are proven to have pervasive effects on holistic health and wellbeing across the life trajectory. Burke Harris et al. (2018: 1) explain that ACEs are stressful or traumatic events experienced before the age of 18 years. Almost half the population of England and Wales have experienced one ACE as a child and one in 10 individuals have suffered four or more ACEs (Bellis et al., 2014).

The narrative around ACEs began in the late 1990s – predominantly as a result of a ground-breaking, longitudinal study, conducted by Dr Felitti and his colleagues in 1998. The article, published in *The American Journal of Preventive Medicine*, remains the most cited article in that journal's history.

The majority of the 286 interviews that Felitti and his colleagues conducted as part of their research, evidenced childhood sexual abuse. This led them to answer one of the questions that had troubled them for so long concerning the obesity programme at Felitti's clinic – these individuals used food as a comfort to counteract feelings of anxiety, fear and depression that were caused by the abuse they were subjected to. Not eating the food meant no comfort, no escape from the psychological pain. To these patients, being obese was not the problem – it was the antidote to the suffering.

Following this revelation, Felitti and his colleagues researched childhood trauma, adding questions concerning childhood experiences, current behaviours and holistic health, in two types of confidential questionnaires distributed among the 17,424 individuals – each designed for men and women respectively. Based on the questionnaire responses, individuals were scored on their ACEs: the more ACEs they endured, the higher their ACEs score – the higher their ACEs score, the increased likelihood of risk-taking behaviours, chronic ill-health and premature death. This will be explored in the following section.

DOI: 10.4324/b23180-7

Felitti and his colleagues contributed to the definition of ACEs that is commonly referred to across the education, health care and criminal justice systems today. The 10 ACEs identified, which underpin their 1998 ACEs study, fall under the toxic trio of:

1 **Abuse**
   Emotional abuse
   Physical abuse
   Sexual abuse

2 **Neglect**
   Emotional neglect
   Physical neglect

3 **Household Challenges (or Dysfunction)**
   Domestic abuse (or domestic violence)
   Substance abuse
   Mental illness
   Parental separation/divorce
   Incarcerated parent/relative.

In the story, you will note that Maya is exposed to ACEs such as having an incarcerated parent, witnessing frequent, violent arguments at home and being picked on at school (or bullying – which is not actually identified in the original ACEs study – but is now widely accepted as a traumatic experience).

The 10 ACEs are depicted below, in The **10 ACEs**.

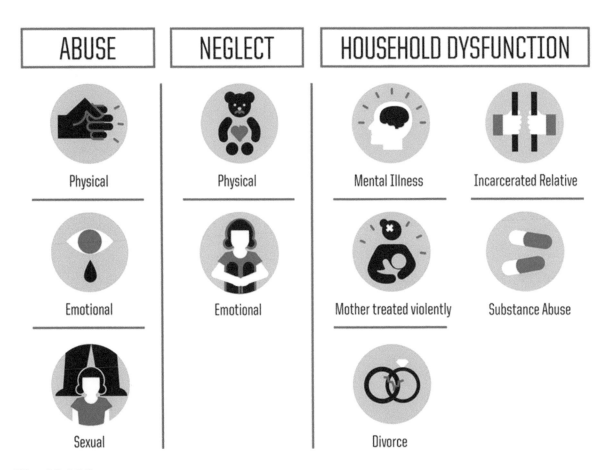

The 10 ACEs
Adapted from Centers for Disease Control and Prevention (2020).

As just mentioned and what is evident from looking at these ACEs, is that not every potential negative experience is identified. This is because the emphasis is on the child's direct experiences in the home. This means that relevant factors which may actually *cause* ACEs such as parental/caregiver childhood abuse do not feature – along with adverse experiences such as bullying, community violence, natural disasters, war, displacement, poverty/economic hardship, oppression and racism – each of which is highly likely to exert pervasive negative effects on the child and their family.

The Long-Term Impact of ACEs on Health and Wellbeing Across the Life Trajectory

Adopting a whole-life perspective, findings from the landmark study demonstrated an unequivocal connection between the length, severity and cumulative effects of ACEs and multiple risk factors for several of the leading causes of death in adults, including:

- Chronic obstructive pulmonary disease
- Asthma
- Obesity
- Kidney disease
- Stroke
- Coronary heart disease
- Cancer
- Diabetes
- Substance abuse
- Violence
- Imprisonment.

(Centers for Disease Control and Prevention, 2020; Seeman, et al., 2010; Felitti, et al., 1998).

The impact of ACEs also tends to include poor general health, difficulty in self-regulating emotions and behaviour, nightmares, sleep disturbances, increased absences from nursery/school/college, learning difficulties, violent behaviours (such as self-harming, weapon-carrying, physical fighting, bullying and in young people, dating violence) and suicide-related behaviours.

The image, **The Impact of ACEs on Health and Wellbeing Across the Life Trajectory**, below, illustrates this whole life perspective, which starts with ACEs at the bottom, leading to derailed healthy brain development, diminished holistic development and wellbeing, engagement in health-harming behaviours, such as smoking, harmful alcohol consumption and drug use, to possible premature death – with individuals who have six or more ACEs potentially dying up to 20 years earlier than an individual who has no ACEs (Hughes et al., 2017; Brown et al., 2009).

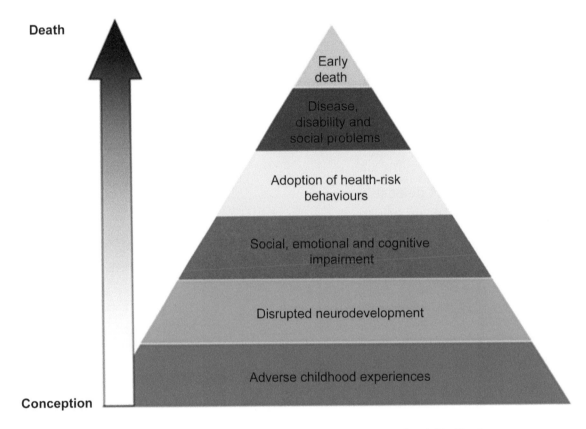

The Impact of ACEs on Health and Wellbeing Across the Life Trajectory

ACEs – Proceed with Caution!

The ACEs movement is now more widely understood and used as a central part of the narrative around early childhood adversity on a global scale. The children's storybook and this guide are part of this narrative, helping to raise awareness and instigate positive action. However, it is important to acknowledge that the ACEs movement is not without its critiques. It is important for you to understand the rationale underlying the critiques to build an informed and balanced opinion.

Before you read on, it is worth bearing in mind that each of the critiques is only introduced in brief. For further information on these critiques of ACEs, you may wish to refer to my book, *The Neuroscience of the Developing Child. Self-Regulation for Wellbeing and a Sustainable Future* (please see Bibliography).

Critiques of the ACEs Movement

The landmark ACEs study and consequent theoretical frameworks have been immensely beneficial and helpful in raising awareness of the persistent, global menace of abuse and neglect. Individuals who suffered adversity during childhood, at last had something to identify with, something that offered a representation of these experiences and perhaps even some explanation as to why they behave the way they do. However, the original ACEs study (Felitti et al., 1998) and some of its successors, continue to be heavily critiqued for diverse reasons, some of which will be discussed in the following sections. *While reading, it will be useful for you to form a balanced opinion of your own, based on the advantages and disadvantages posed by the ACEs movement.*

Narrow in Focus

When we reflect on the complexity of life and all it brings, we know that more than 10 types of adversity exist – yet only 10 ACEs form the basis of the original theoretical framework. This means that if an individual has suffered any of the aforementioned ACEs, such as bullying, oppression, racism, community violence or war, they

DOI: 10.4324/b23180-8

technically have no ACEs because they are not listed in the framework. Thus, when a framework such as this is so narrow – or incomplete in the insight and explanations it provides – it could be argued that it therefore cannot be reliably used as a framework from which similar studies could be conducted.

Pathologization of Early Adversity

The ACEs framework is considered by some (Kelly-Irving and Delpierre, 2019; Taylor-Robinson et al., 2018) to encourage the pathologization of those who were exposed to ACEs. In simple terms, this means that these survivors are seen to have a problem, illness or "disorder" that requires a medical intervention to treat it – typically, anti-depressants, anti-psychotics and medication for anxiety. It is important to hold in mind that children can be incredibly resilient and with the right, timely interventions, their outcomes need not be determined by an assessment tool that was used on a non-representative, homogenous group.

ACEs Scores – What's the Score?

Using deterministic frameworks which seek to quantify the experience of adversity through a point-scoring system, was indeed an effective way to capture vast amounts of data concerning ACEs, to list them and help bring them to the attention of the public. They are, however, a crude way of collating data on some of the most atrocious wrongdoings against children and adolescents and should not be used by the layperson to make predictions based on ACEs scores.

Scoring systems will fail us. Our experiences are too diverse to be categorized – as are we.

ACEs Are Not Destiny – Why We Are Not Defined by Our Trauma

While the detrimental health and behavioural ACEs outcomes continue to be reliably demonstrated across studies internationally, if an individual's fate is therefore already written, there would be no point in even attempting to rebuild a life, following trauma. We know that this is not the case for everyone who was exposed to ACEs. For those of us who, for example, work in teaching, healthcare, social care and therapeutic services, we understand and believe in the potential for healing and positive change. The brain's life-long plasticity is testament to this fact: neural pathways develop, grow and strengthen in response to experiences. When these experiences and relationships are responsive, protective and enabling, this directly impacts the brain's architecture, laying a robust foundation for subsequent brain development.

What is critical in terms of healing and recovery from ACEs and trauma, is the presence of protective factors (counter-ACEs or buffers) – which we see plenty of in the story. These protective factors are explored in the following chapter.

Children *Can* Overcome Their ACEs – How Protective Factors Can Help

Protective factors can do much to minimize the negative impact of early adversity. Over time, they can help the child to feel loved, valued and respected, while building the child's sense of self-worth and resilience. Ultimately, protective factors help children to break free from the associated harmful stereotypes and narratives bestowed upon them by such methods of assessment. *We are not our trauma and it need not define who we become.*

Take a look at the image below. It identifies just some of the protective factors that help to minimize the impact of ACEs.

Protective Factors for Children Exposed to ACEs

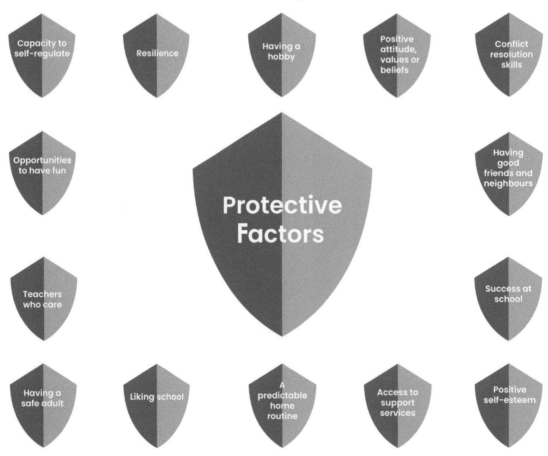

Protective Factors

DOI: 10.4324/b23180-9

As identified, having at least one person the child feels safe with, whom they can trust and is consistent in their unconditional positive regard for them, can do much to help minimize the devastating impact of ACEs. It shows them that they are worthy of love and care and that there are good people in the world, while providing them with a much- needed positive role model. This might be a teacher, assistant, relative, foster carer or a health care practitioner the child sees on a regular basis. The consistency, patience and healthy relationship they provide, over time, not only help to build the child's resilience, but also strengthen their social and emotional skills, while equipping them to build a more positive view of themselves – one where they can feel seen, important and liked – or as Dr Siegel (Siegel and Bryson, 2012) says:

- ✔ Seen
- ✔ Safe
- ✔ Soothed
- ✔ Secure.

Think back to Maya in the story. She has many protective factors in her life, which she is able to identify towards the end of story. As she writes these down in her journal, she begins to feel more resilient – and happy.

What other protective factors can you think of? Encourage the children you support, to think of any in their lives. Where possible, encourage the creation of protective factors in their lives. Depending on local provision available and what they are permitted to do, it might be getting a small pet, joining a drama or art club or speaking with their family about the possibility of play-based therapy (depending on the child's needs).

Now that we have looked at ACEs and their impact on holistic wellbeing, we will explore their impact on the developing brain and consequent behaviour.

The Brilliant Brain

Now that we have looked at ACEs and how they impact a child's holistic wellbeing, we will take a closer look at the developing brain and what happens to this during toxic stress.

It weighs approximately 3.3 pounds (generally a little less for female adult brains), is pinkish-brown in colour, has the texture of a firm jelly and resides in your skull – welcome to your brilliant brain!

It might not sound so awe-inspiring in that brief description, but the human brain controls everything we think, feel and do. It is the seat of rationality, creativity and imagination and holds the key to consciousness. Along with other key organs, it keeps us alive – and we may never get to fully understand this astonishing organ and the secrets it holds.

At birth, a baby's brain weighs approximately 350 to 400 grams (three-quarters of a pound) and contains roughly 86 billion neurons (brain cells)!

Repeated Early Experiences Strengthen Neural Pathways

A neural pathway is a series of connected neurons that sends signals from one part of the brain to another. Think of a physical pathway – if you keep using the same route, you can remember it almost automatically. Neural pathways work in this way. The more something is done, the better neurons in different parts of the brain become at remembering what to do and anticipating what will happen next.

Early childhood is a critical time to lay down these neural pathways. However, not all pathways are beneficial. Unfortunately, due to negative experiences, some pathways that are laid down in this period are unhealthy and these negatively impact a child's understanding of the world around them. For example, being regularly ignored, humiliated or even reprimanded when in distress, can make a child fearful and distrustful of others.

The Brain's Emotion Centre – The Limbic System

The limbic system is situated deep in the centre of the brain. It is a collection of structures that are heavily involved in triggering our emotional and behavioural

DOI: 10.4324/b23180-10

responses. Powerful emotions such as anger, sadness, envy and joy are all activated in this region of the brain. It also plays an important role in regulating our mood and levels of motivation. For these reasons, the limbic system is sometimes called the "emotional brain". Our limbic system is mainly involuntary (unconscious), often causing us to act before we are able to think. This is because a great deal of sensory information (what we can see, smell and hear) passes through the limbic system first before being processed in the decision-making areas of the brain (the frontal lobes). If this sensory information is deemed a threat or too overwhelming, the limbic system activates the body's fight-or-flight response. For young children, a "threat" might simply be something like not wanting to share a toy or falling out with a friend.

The limbic system performs many vital functions. Part of the limbic system helps the brain to process and store memories, which means that it aids our ability to retain and recall information (which is key to learning). Our stress response (how we respond to potential or perceived threats and stressful situations) also begins in the limbic system. It helps us to survive by regulating several essential physiological functions, such as our breathing, heart rate and appetite. Illustrated in the image below, **The Limbic System**, you can see some of the key components of the limbic system.

The Limbic System

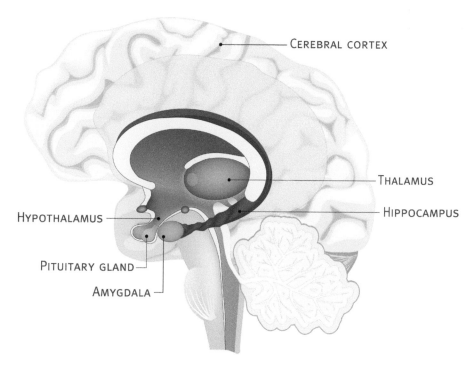

The Limbic System

- **The amygdala** – (pronounced uh-mig-duh-luh) plays a central role in our emotional responses. It also acts like the brain's "panic button". It is activated when we feel frightened, angry or anxious and automatically triggers our fight-or-flight response by sending signals to other parts of the limbic system to release stress hormones that prepare the body to fight or run away. A child's behaviour during fight-or-flight might look like them screaming, crying, hurting others or themselves

- **The hippocampus** – looking a little bit like a seahorse, this structure is the memory centre – or filing cabinet – of the brain. It forms, organizes and stores new memories. It also helps us to associate memories with various senses. For example, the smell of gingerbread might remind some people of Christmas. The hippocampus would process this memory and store it deep in the brain

- **The thalamus** – this acts as a kind of "pit stop" for motor and sensory information. For example, sensory impulses travel from the surface of the body towards the thalamus, which receives them as sensations. These sensations are then passed to the surface of the brain for interpretation

- **The hypothalamus** – works with the adjoining pituitary gland to produce several important hormones (chemical messengers) and to release these into the brain and bloodstream. For example, the stress hormone cortisol is produced by the hypothalamus in response to physical and emotional stress. The hypothalamus also helps to maintain our body's internal balance by regulating our blood pressure and heart rate, as well as our breathing, body temperature, appetite, thirst and sleep cycles.

The "Upstairs" and "Downstairs" Brain

The concept of the "upstairs" and "downstairs" brain was developed by the American neuroscientist Dr Daniel Siegel (Siegel and Bryson, 2012) as part of his Hand Model of the Brain. Although it may sound simplistic, it is a very effective way of understanding the relationship between the cerebral cortex (the surface layer of the brain) and the limbic system and how the two work together (or not) in young children.

Imagine your brain is a two-storey house. The "upstairs" brain comprises of the four lobes of the brain – the frontal, temporal, parietal and occipital lobes – and the thin cerebral cortex that covers each of these. Of particular importance is the frontal lobe, specifically its prefrontal cortex (PFC) – this brain region resides directly behind the eyes and the forehead (as shown in the image below).

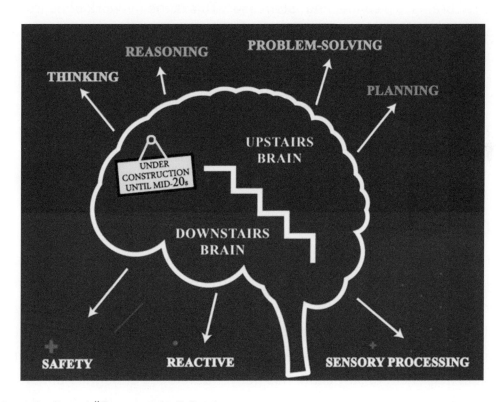

The "Upstairs" and "Downstairs" Brain
Adapted from Greg Santucci (2021).
Concept from *The Whole Brain Child*, by Dr Daniel Siegel and Dr Tina Payne Bryson (2012).

DOI: 10.4324/b23180-11

Did you know? The PFC takes a very long time to be fully developed. Researchers believe it takes approximately 25 years! (The PFC is highlighted in yellow in the image above).

Think about this in relation to how much we demand of children in terms of being able to cope with the stressors in their lives and doing well at school. We expect far too much, without effectively supporting them to be able to overcome these stressors, in order to be *able* to learn.

As stated, the PFC is responsible for our executive functioning skills – our ability to focus, plan, prioritize, reason and make rational decisions. It also helps us to become more self-aware and aware of others.

The "downstairs" brain refers to the lower regions of the brain, including the limbic system. As you learned earlier, the limbic system is responsible for some critical functions that keep us alive (like breathing and regulating our heart rate) as well as our impulses and emotions (like anger and fear). Between the "upstairs" and "downstairs" brains is a connecting "staircase". This is the network of neurons and synapses that carry information up and down, to and from the different parts of the brain. Both areas of our brain need to work together for us to function well. However, young children's "upstairs" and "downstairs" brains often struggle to work together – and this is why so many children who have been exposed to early adversity tend to struggle to do well in school, because while they are functioning from their emotionally reactive, "downstairs" brain, their thinking, "upstairs" brain cannot come online.

What Causes This?

1 On the one hand, the executive functions of the "upstairs" brain needs a set of skills (such as focusing, planning, prioritizing, reasoning and making rational decisions) which takes time to develop. On the other hand, the limbic system of the "downstairs" brain develops much more quickly. Therefore, when a child perceives a threat or becomes angry, the "upstairs" part of the brain, which should help them to stay calm, has not yet developed enough to understand and restrain the powerful emotional reactions created in the "downstairs" brain's limbic system

2 The stress hormones (primarily cortisol and adrenaline) that are released in the "downstairs" brain during the fight-or-flight response often stop

messages from getting through to the "upstairs" brain. In other words, the staircase becomes cluttered. This happens in adults too. Put simply, the stress hormones can prevent us from accessing our "upstairs" brain, which is key in helping us to think clearly and rationally. More on this shortly.

Both of these factors may cause children to become dysregulated (in other words, become deeply upset or angry or have a marked change in mood) and show behaviours that may challenge others while overwhelming themselves.

Dr Dan Siegel uses another concept as part of the "upstairs" and "downstairs" brain to explain what happens when the reasoning part of the brain (the PFC) is unable to control the powerful emotions coming from down below in the limbic system. He calls this "flipping the lid," and it is an idea that is becoming more widely used in the training of EY practitioners. It is also a useful way of helping children to understand why they get angry (for example) and perhaps react in ways that further dysregulate them.

The "lid flips" when the amygdala (the brain's "panic button") is activated and a child's upstairs brain loses all control of the "downstairs brain". This can happen in just a few seconds and can be due to a range of reasons: a child might have had a disagreement with their friend, be feeling sad or angry at being told off for not paying attention in class. When this happens, the child metaphorically "flips their lid", and there is an explosion of emotion (which then directs their behaviour).

There are various YouTube clips available where you can watch Dan Siegel explaining his Hand Model of the Brain in more detail. Here are some examples:

Dr Daniel Siegel's Hand Model of the Brain (www.youtube.com/watch?v=f-m2Ycd MdFw)

Daniel Siegel – "'Flipping Your Lid:' A Scientific Explanation" (www.youtube. com/watch?v=G0T_2NNoC68)

Adults can also "flip their lid", so the same model can also be applied to parenting and coping with stress in the workplace, for example:

Daniel Siegel's Hand Model of the Brain (www.youtube.com/watch?v=qFTljLo1bK8)

When a child "flips their lid," their behaviour is often labelled by adults as "naughty" or "challenging", and the child might be reprimanded or punished in some way (told to take a "time out", for example). However, this is a missed opportunity and is psychologically damaging to the child (Kohn, 2018). What the child really needs in this moment is CR from an adult to help them return to a safe psychological state while enabling them to learn from the experience. Put simply, CR is a relational, supportive process between a caring adult and the child, which builds SR skills. This will also teach them how to manage in similar situations in the future – ultimately, to self-regulate.

The "flipping lid" concept and the Hand Model of the Brain help to explain why a child who feels threatened or anxious can find it incredibly difficult to regulate their emotions and subsequent behaviour. Parents, primary carers, EY practitioners and teachers are incredibly important during this process of CR. They can help children to become more aware of their emotions and teach them strategies that help them to remain calm while their "upstairs" brain catches up and, to use another analogy, "comes back online". See the chapter, **The Invaluable Role of Co-Regulation**, for further discussion of CR.

Self-Regulation – What Is It and Why Is It Important?

At its simplest, SR is our ability to regulate (or manage) our thoughts, feelings and behaviour. Being able to self-regulate helps us to remain calm and attentive. It also helps us to respond, rather than react (often without thinking, in unhelpful ways), when faced with stressors and strong emotions.

Without SR, children struggle to develop meaningful relationships, communicate effectively, succeed at school or thrive personally. This makes sense when we reflect on SR in the context of its 10 attributes, listed below:

- ✔ Managing own feelings and behaviours
- ✔ Self-soothing/bouncing back from upset
- ✔ Being able to curb impulsive behaviours
- ✔ Being able to concentrate on a task
- ✔ Being able to ignore distractions
- ✔ Behaving in ways that are prosocial (like empathizing and getting along with others)
- ✔ Planning
- ✔ Thinking before acting
- ✔ Delaying gratification
- ✔ Persisting in the face of difficulty.

When a child can self-regulate, they are able to think before they act and self-calm when they are met with overwhelming or stressful input. Think back to when Maya feels angry, hurt and frustrated in the story – she slams her bedroom door, pushes a child to the ground and shouts. Yet, as the story progresses, we see that with adult understanding of her dysregulated behaviours and consistent CR, these dysregulated behaviours develop into behaviours which are more self-regulated and actually help Maya to feel calmer and see the positive in situations. We go on to see

DOI: 10.4324/b23180-12

her doing (among other things) in-the-moment deep breathing, speaking with her parents about how she feels and journaling.

The Five Domains of Self-Regulation

In order to develop a robust understanding of SR, it is important to understand that it is not a one-dimensional skill that resides in just one part of the body or brain region. According to Shanker (2020), there are five domains of SR – each affecting the other and each with its unique stressors. These domains are vital to hold in mind when trying to figure out the root cause of children's (and young adults') emotional responses and consequent behaviours – as opposed to only reacting to the surface behaviours we see – which is sadly what all too often happens. Take a look at the table, **The Five Domains of Self-Regulation,** below and reflect on the triggers. Some may bring to mind triggers in your provision that you previously did not think posed a problem – some may bring to mind Maya's triggers in the story.

The list of triggers in the table below is not exhaustive but instead serves as a catalyst for further thinking about the children you might support who have been exposed to ACEs and how you and your team could better meet their needs.

The Five Domains of Self-Regulation

Domain	Stressors
Biological domain 	This domain focuses on physical health and wellbeing. Stressors include insufficient sleep, poor diet, physical abuse, having to be sat still for extended periods, lack of exercise, lack of fresh air, excessive or low energy levels, illness, pain, sensitivity to certain fabrics (clothing), excessive visual stimulation (brightly coloured wall displays and hanging displays), bright lighting and feeling too hot or cold
Emotional domain 	This includes a child's ability to monitor, consider and (as a result) change their behaviour. Stressors affecting this domain include abuse, trauma, bullying, bereavement, transitions, changes in routine, feeling embarrassed, unwelcomed, anxious, depressed or scared. It also includes difficulty in coping with strong emotions – both positive (such as excitement) and negative (such as anger)

Domain	Stressors
Cognitive domain 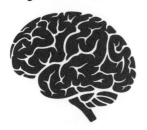	This domain involves the mental processes involved in building knowledge, such as paying attention, perception, memory and problem-solving. Difficulties in the other domains will impact a child's ability to pay attention, which often gets them in trouble at school. Stressors include abuse, lack of intellectual stimulation, confusion, difficulty concentrating, difficulty in prioritizing tasks, poor memory and low frustration tolerance
Social domain 	This includes verbal and non-verbal communication, empathy, active listening, managing friendships and overcoming conflict. Stressors include abuse, a lack of friends, being isolated or bullied at school, not having anyone to play with during break times, difficulty in understanding social norms and understanding the impact of own behaviour on others, feeling awkward in social situations, large groups, disagreements and feeling defensive
Prosocial domain 	This includes the capacity to care about others' feelings and to help them manage their feelings – to co-regulate them during emotionally charged times. Stressors include abuse, difficulty reading others' cues, difficulty coping with other people's stress, sharing, telling the truth and knowing right from wrong. It also includes injustice, unfairness, expectations of others, being late and being exploited by others.

A Word on Dysregulation – It Is Not a Tantrum!

As we saw throughout the story, there were times when Maya felt sad, upset and angry – which resulted in her becoming *dysregulated*. This means that she was unable to manage her emotions and behaviours and ended up with a rapid heartbeat, nausea, crying, shouting and withdrawing in times of panic and stress. Too often, people call this dysregulated behaviour a tantrum.

So, how is a tantrum generally defined? Take a look at the few examples below.

The online Oxford Learner's Dictionary (2022) defines it as:

> A sudden short period of angry, unreasonable behaviour, especially in a child – to have/throw a tantrum.

The online Cambridge Dictionary (2022) explains that a tantrum is:

> A sudden period of uncontrolled anger like a young child's ...

While the internationally popular free online encyclopaedia, Wikipedia (2022) explains that:

> A tantrum, temper tantrum, meltdown, fit or hissy fit is an emotional outburst ... typically characterised by stubbornness, crying, screaming, violence, defiance, angry ranting, a resistance to attempts at pacification ... Throwing a temper tantrum can lead to a child getting detention or being suspended from school, for older school age children.

How do these definitions make you feel, as someone who might have children or work with children?

The term tantrum is inaccurate, disrespectful and dismissive of the child's psychological state in-the-moment. We should all therefore make the effort to use the correct and more respectful term concerning such stress behaviours, *dysregulation*.

What Might Dysregulated Behaviour Look Like?

Signs of dysregulation will of course vary, depending on the individual child, their age and their triggers, but some dysregulated behaviours might include:

- Becoming angry or frustrated quickly
- Crying
- Harming themselves or others
- High levels of anxiety
- Inability to be flexible
- Refusing to speak
- Withdrawing
- Struggling with transitions between activities

Maya Feeling Angry

- Having difficulty waiting or taking turns

- Grabbing or touching objects impulsively

- Struggling with being in close proximity to others (for example, circle time)

- Demonstrating difficulties and frustration during social interactions (for example, talking too loudly, standing too close or touching others).

During dysregulated moments, it is critical to understand that none of the child's emotions are "bad" – and that actually, the child is dysregulated – as opposed to "having a tantrum".

It is important to hold in mind that the language we use influences our responses to the child's dysregulated behaviour, so it will also be important to eschew all things behaviour management – this means no more reward charts, time out, removal of "golden time", detention, suspension, expulsion and certainly no punishments – physical or otherwise. These only serve to demoralize the child through (public) shaming.

Let us think back to Maya's dysregulated moments. Maya's mother responded to her calmly and affectionately. She listened to Maya and tried to reassure her, to make her feel better – in other words, she co-regulated her emotions and behaviour. What might have resulted if her mother had punished her instead?

This state of emotional dysregulation is what causes a child – or adult to "flip their lid" (discussed earlier) – and when we permit ourselves to reframe the behaviour and the underpinning neurobiology of stress behaviours, we are equipping them to better manage their emotions and behaviour throughout their lives. This leads us to the iceberg of behaviour.

Understanding Behaviour – What Lies Beneath

When you reflect on those behaviours that typically present as "frustrating" or "challenging", do you consider the possible causes of the behaviours? Or do you dive right in with the behaviour management policy and threaten to reprimand the dysregulated child? ACEs have a direct impact on behaviour, but there remains a lack of understanding of this – and how to support a child when they are dysregulated.

Viewing the child through the lens of SR enables us to think that bit deeper about behaviour and *reframe* what we see. It equips us to understand that beneath anger, might be sadness; beneath aggression might be shame and humiliation. It is therefore helpful to think of behaviour as being similar to an iceberg – with the tip of the iceberg including those behaviours we can see children (or young adults) engage in, while beneath the surface of the water are the *emotional causes* of the behaviours and unmet needs.

If you do not already do so, it would be helpful to have these conversations with the adults in the child's life to enable them to be more curious, considerate and compassionate about the child's behaviours, as opposed to focusing on the "need" to discipline them for behaving in ways that they have minimal, if any, control of.

The Iceberg of Behaviour, below, outlines just a few commonly encountered behaviours that are deemed to be challenging (at its tip), with some possible underlying causes of these behaviours that we do not see, beneath its surface.

The Iceberg of Behaviour

We must never take anything at face value, because as we know, children's behaviour is communication – not misbehaviour. The younger the child, the more reliant they will be on actions, as opposed to expressing themselves verbally.

This is all the more important to hold in mind when it comes to children who have been exposed to ACEs. All too often, these children will have unmet needs around:

- Their basic physical safety
- Their psychological safety
- Companionship
- Healthy attachments
- Healthy boundaries
- Positive role models
- Others' positive expectations of them
- Feeling acknowledged, needed, valued and loved.

So, the next time you are met with behaviours that you might have previously viewed as "challenging", "wilful" or "defiant", first pause to think about what might be going on beneath what you can see – and how you might better support the child to work through their emotions.

If you are in a position to, it might also be helpful to speak with the child's primary carers about the iceberg of behaviour, so that they too are able to respond to their child's behaviours in ways that are *less reactive* and *more understanding*.

The Invaluable Role of Co-Regulation in Helping Children to Self-Regulate

As mentioned in the chapter, **The "Upstairs" and "Downstairs" Brain**, CR is a *relational*, supportive process between a caring adult and the child, which builds SR – across the lifespan. This means it is an approach to interacting with the child that prioritises the *relationship between the adult and child*. This includes the adult:

- ✔ Showing respect

- ✔ Helping the child to feel psychologically and physically safe

- ✔ Active listening

- ✔ Being genuine

- ✔ Reflecting back to the child what they are trying to tell the adult

- ✔ Keeping calm

- ✔ Being patient

- ✔ Empathizing

- ✔ Problem-solving with the child.

When done effectively, it is a swift, in-the-moment way to help calm a dysregulated child. When we co-regulate a child's emotions and behaviour, this certainly means *not* reprimanding the child, shouting at them, or issuing any threats of punishment or consequences.

Easy as 1, 2, 3! The Three Main Approaches to Co-Regulation

When it comes to co-regulating children's emotions and behaviour, there exist many approaches to our co-regulatory relationships, the resources we choose to use and the environments that we choose to provide. To make it a little easier to reflect on

DOI: 10.4324/b23180-13

some of these, this guide refers to Rosanbalm and Murray (2017), who indicate the following three main approaches to achieving CR:

1 The provision of warm and responsive relationships
2 Through the teaching and modelling of SR skills
3 The structure of the indoor and outdoor environments.

This is illustrated below in **The Three Approaches to Achieving Co-Regulation**.

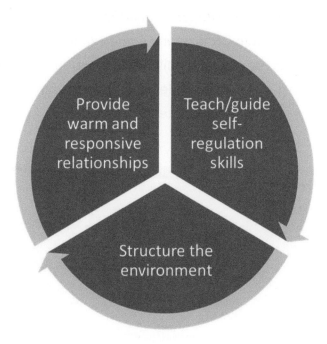

The Three Approaches to Achieving Co-Regulation

Each approach will mean something different to everyone, depending on factors including (but not exclusive to):

- The type of setting
- The structure of the indoor and outdoor environments
- The age of children cared for
- The adults' temperament
- The children's temperament
- The level of CR children receive from their primary carers
- The presence of any special educational needs or disability (SEND)
- The emotional availability of the adults at the time.

Each of the three approaches will now be examined in turn. They are packed with practical strategies that are immediately actionable, so, if you do not already, make a plan of how you will action these as part of your provision.

1 The Provision of Warm and Responsive Relationships

You set the foundations for SR to be possible and while each of the three approaches are equally important, getting those warm and responsive relationships in place, as *the* foundation of your ever-evolving, co-regulatory support is vital in ensuring an ethos of nurturing SR through CR is in place and experienced by everyone in the setting. The main aim of co-regulating a child's thoughts, feelings and behaviour is to equip them to move from a state of dependency to independence – that is, to master the ability to self-regulate. This is highlighted in **The CO-REG Acronym**, below.

Effective ways to...

Communicate - Think about your words and body language when trying to soothe the child. Make sure you are at the child's level and that you are speaking calmly and slowly

Observe - Look out for any triggers in the environment or during interactions, so that you are better able to prevent these from presenting issues in the first instance

Reason - Once you have helped the child to calm down, talk about alternative ways they could respond the next time they become dysregulated and why this is important to do

Empathise - By listening, showing understanding and validating their feelings. You can do this by reflecting back what they tell you: "I understand that you're feeling angry"

Guide - Talk the child through in-the-moment strategies that they can use to calm down. This might include breathing exercises, grounding techniques, or sitting in a quiet space

We co-regulate a child's thoughts, feelings and behaviour in order to nurture their ability to self-regulate, so that they can move from dependency to independence.

Dr Mine Conkbayir

The CO-REG Acronym

Providing CR should not only take place when a child is dysregulated, but instead, infuse all interactions between adults and children as much as possible. That is not to say that we must co-regulate all the time, but that we must endeavour to, as regularly and consistently as is possible.

What might these interactions look like as part of those warm and responsive relationships?

The Three Rs

Children who have been exposed to ACEs might find it difficult to behave in ways that safely draw adults close to them to build relationships and ensure their needs are met. Instead, they are often misrepresented as being "attention-seeking" or "acting out", with adults pushing further away from them. Really, all they want and need is companionship; someone to care about them, their needs, fears and hopes. They will need focused support and positive modelling of how to engage in and enjoy healthy ways of interacting – ways that are not intended to psychologically undermine or humiliate others, where each person is listening and being listened to, with their thoughts and feelings respected.

In this regard, it might be helpful to consider **the three Rs (respectful and responsive relationships)**. The three Rs enable children to learn about their world and their place in it, through first-hand experience of reciprocal interactions which require them to use their emergent cognitive, physical, language, social and emotional skills as they engage with a responsive adult. This adult observes their cues, engages with and responds to them in ways that are timely, authentic and useful in identifying their emotions and helping them to self-regulate.

To achieve the three Rs, you also need to:

- Involve children in decisions that affect them

- Validate their emotions

- Explain what you are doing and why

- Adjust your tone of voice and pace of talking to their level

- Take the time to read their cues and respond in ways that help them feel listened to and valued.

Reflect on the three Rs and Maya in the story – although the main adults in her life often behave in ways that leave her feeling very upset and angry, they also give her the time and space to talk about how she is feeling; they show Maya genuine concern and respect; they encourage her to express her emotions in ways that are safe and they ask open-ended questions which encourage her to find the solutions to what is bothering her at the time.

Open-ended questions are questions that the adult asks the child to encourage discussion, to express safely how they are feeling and ultimately, to help them calm down. Unlike closed questions, like "are you ok?" or "do you need help?", they get more than a one-word answer which is usually "yes" or "no".

Below are just a few opening statements that you could use to encourage a conversation with the child, based on the behaviours you might observe (obviously, you should adapt these as necessary):

- ✔ I can see you look very upset. What happened?
- ✔ I understand that made you feel angry. I would feel angry too
- ✔ I noticed you got cross when you had to come in after outdoor play
- ✔ It's ok to feel frustrated, but it's not ok to hit or shout at our friends.
- ✔ What could you do the next time you feel frustrated?
- ✔ What can I do to help you feel better?

When used in ways that are appropriate to the child's stage of understanding, such interactions can be effective in not only developing their prosocial skills, but also in building their ability to discuss, reason and solve problems (all those "upstairs" brain skills).

2   Teaching and Modelling of Self-Regulation Skills

Children who have been exposed to ACEs are likely to be triggered frequently and on a daily basis (across those five domains of SR). This is commonly due to not having been provided with a healthy role model for SR by their primary carers and being in a state of chronic hyper-arousal as a result of the exposure to the toxic stressors in their lives. They will therefore need adults who can identify and minimize the presence of these triggers, while being confident in co-regulating them when they do become dysregulated.

How is this relevant to you? Put simply, **you cannot co-regulate, if you cannot self-regulate**. Children who have been exposed to ACEs *need* the presence of an adult who can "hold space" (be physically, mentally and emotionally present) with them during times of need – as well as provide a positive role model for companionship in general. Although realistically, none of us are calm and emotionally present all of the time, providing a foundation of unconditional regard and responsive care that is generally consistent and predictable is vital in equipping children with the practical in-the-moment strategies to use when they are feeling dysregulated (which we will look at further on). As the child grows older and matures intellectually, these strategies will develop with them.

Before we examine some tried and tested CR strategies, let us focus on *you*. Read on to see how you fare when it comes to self-regulating your emotions and behaviour during emotionally charged, or difficult times.

Self-Regulation – Do You Sink or Swim?

While we all have "off-days", with minimum capacity to stay calm and support others, if this is our norm, we will not be best positioned to co-regulate. In fact, we will probably end up "adding fuel to the fire" – making things worse. Moreover, left unresolved, poor SR *will* have a long-term negative impact on psychological and physiological health, with potentially compromised ability to build and maintain personal and professional relationships and dependence on alcohol, cigarettes and recreational drugs to self-soothe in the absence of self-regulatory capacity.

So, how do *you* fare when it comes to self-regulating – particularly during stressful moments? This leads us to your journey along the *Stream of Self-Regulation.*

The Stream of Self-Regulation

This **Stream of Self-Regulation** (below) provides a quick and easy way for you to identify how effectively you self-regulate your emotions and behaviour. This can then help you to work on any areas that you feel need to be developed so that you are better able to self-regulate, as well as enhance your role as co-regulator. The Stream helps to raise your *self-awareness* and ability to *reflect* on any areas that you might need to work on, without the inclusion of numbers and scales, so as to remove any pressure of scoring points. It is a simple tool with recommended strategies to help you easily navigate your way through your personal SR journey. (One of the strategies referred to, the *Keep Your Cool Toolbox,* is an award-winning, free SR app that I designed. Its website address can be found in the Bibliography).

Take a look and answer the questions that follow.

The Stream of Self-Regulation

When it comes to self-regulating your emotions and behaviour, do you feel like you are sinking or swimming?

This Stream of Self-Regulation provides an easy way for you to identify how effectively you self-regulate. It helps to raise your self-awareness and ability to reflect on any areas that you might need to work on, so that you can stay calm during emotionally charged situations. Practical strategies are provided to help you navigate your self-regulation journey.

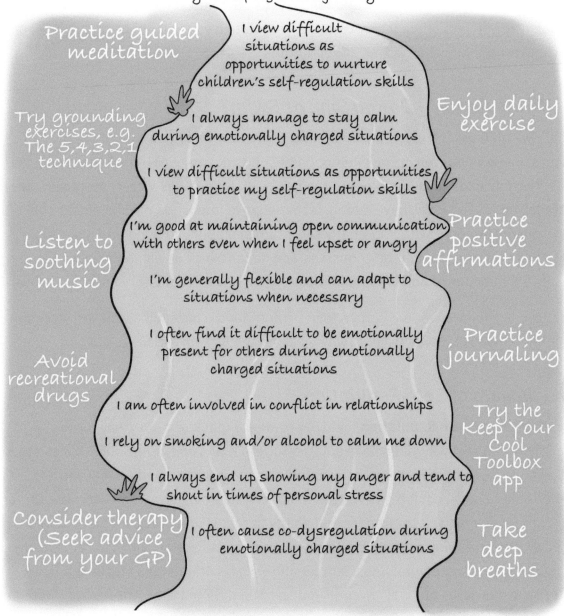

Practice guided meditation

I view difficult situations as opportunities to nurture children's self-regulation skills

Enjoy daily exercise

Try grounding exercises, e.g. The 5,4,3,2,1 technique

I always manage to stay calm during emotionally charged situations

I view difficult situations as opportunities to practice my self-regulation skills

I'm good at maintaining open communication with others even when I feel upset or angry

Practice positive affirmations

Listen to soothing music

I'm generally flexible and can adapt to situations when necessary

I often find it difficult to be emotionally present for others during emotionally charged situations

Practice journaling

Avoid recreational drugs

I am often involved in conflict in relationships

I rely on smoking and/or alcohol to calm me down

Try the Keep Your Cool Toolbox app

I always end up showing my anger and tend to shout in times of personal stress

Consider therapy (Seek advice from your GP)

I often cause co-dysregulation during emotionally charged situations

Take deep breaths

The Stream of Self-Regulation

Over to You!

1 Read through the Stream of Self-Regulation and reflect honestly about your general ability to self-regulate in challenging situations.

    a   Select two statements from the Stream that resonate most with you and explain why.

    b   Are there strategies on the list that you have not tried? Note these down with a view to trying them.

2 What do you understand about the impact of ACEs on a child's ability to self-regulate? Discuss.

3 a   How do you tend to "hold space" for a dysregulated child?

    b   Have there been occasions when you have not managed to do this and co-regulate a child? What were the reasons for this?

    c   What was the outcome? Discuss.

4 In your experience, what are the key characteristics of effective CR and why?

It Takes Two! – Co-Regulation Strategies to Use with Children

We have one job when children are experiencing a heightened state of emotion and that is to help them regulate their feelings so that they are able to reach a state of calm.

Below is a list of just a few in-the-moment CR strategies that you could use to nurture SR skills – some of which will be expanded further on.

✔ **Name it to tame it** – this means acknowledging children's feelings and giving them the names for the emotions they are feeling at the time. For example, in a calm, soothing voice, "I can see you're feeling angry right now". "I would feel angry too. "How can I help you?"

    Identifying and naming those big, overwhelming emotions, can immediately reduce their intensity for the child

✔ **Building SR spaces** – these are cosy spaces which contain a range of objects for a child to use to help them regulate their emotions (further detail provided in the following section, **The Structure of the Indoor and Outdoor Environments**)

✔ **Breathing techniques** – (some ideas are provided further on)

✔ **Glitter jars/sensory bottles** – help to calm and refocus attention. The child gives them a good shake and watches until the glitter settles to the bottom of the jar. Where possible, it is best to make these *with* the child

✔ **Allowing access to comforters when needed** – these provide reassurance and security and must never be taken from the child

✔ **Allowing children to access the outdoors** – helps to "burn off" energy and alleviate hyper/hypo-arousal

✔ **Allowing the child to leave the room when necessary** – the child might benefit from going for a walk, or for some fresh air. (Always ensure that the child is accompanied by an adult)

✔ **Being child-led** – (discussed and agreed between adult and child)

✔ **Suggesting an activity or game which requires turn-taking** – the repetitive actions, talking in a calm voice and distracting the child to focus on, for example, catching the ball, work to regulate them and refocus their attention

✔ **Daily yoga** – reduces arousal, while improving SR and concentration

✔ **Modelling regulated behaviour and ways of interacting** – children look to you as a positive role model. Modelling healthy ways to overcome stressors is vital

✔ **Distraction** – involves gently redirecting the child's focus away from the source of stress in-the-moment. This can swiftly help the child to feel less anxious and more relaxed.

Here are just a few of the listed CR strategies in a little more detail. Reflect on the children you support and what they might respond to best. When planning strategies for the child, it is always best practice to consult *with* the child about what *they* would like to do, while talking about how the experience could help them to better manage their feelings and behaviour – and where possible, always make the effort to engage their primary carers, so that they understand the benefits for the child and that they too are able to do the activities with them.

There are countless breathing techniques to choose from online. A simple online search will yield many results. Here are just a few popular techniques to help get you started.

Calming Cocoa Breathing

This simple breathing exercise is one of many designed to help the child to regulate their breathing when they are feeling dysregulated and need a little help to feel calmer. Give these three easy steps a go with the children you support:

1 Imagine you're holding a cup of delicious hot cocoa, **bringing your cupped hands close to your face**
2 Now imagine you're breathing in its yummy smell, as you take in a **slow, deep breath through your nose**
3 But you can't drink it hot! Imagine you're blowing on it to cool it down, as you **take some slow breaths out**, before you drink the tasty hot cocoa.

Hot Chocolate Breathing

Bubble Breathing

1 Imagine you are trying to blow a really big bubble through a bubble wand. (You can close your eyes if you want – but you do not have to)

2 Now **take a long deep breath in through your nose and hold it for a second or two**

3 Now **breathe out very slowly**, as if you are blowing a huge bubble!

4 Picture the shimmery bubbles floating away, carrying your worries away with them!

5 Repeat this as many times as you need, until you feel more calm.

Bubble Breathing

Developing Self-Regulation – Child's Play?

Play is one of the best ways to help children overcome the impact of ACEs and nurture children's SR skills, as it provides a non-pressurizing medium through which they can:

✔ Regulate their own thinking, by talking to themselves as they play

✔ Test out their skills of cooperating with others

✔ Not give up when faced with challenges

✔ Build patience, such as waiting their turn

✔ Understand the need for rules and follow these

✔ Follow instructions

✔ Build the confidence to talk to children outside of their friendship group

✔ Make and talk through plans with their peers

✔ Overcome disagreements in socially acceptable ways

✔ Focus their attention and remain mentally present in the experience

✔ Filter out distractions

✔ Curb impulses and remain focused on the play

✔ Solve problems independently or in a group.

There are many games that you can play to help develop children's SR. You can adapt well-known games or make up your own, with the child. Take a look at the list below.

Top 10 Play Experiences to Nurture Self-Regulation Skills:

1 **Board games** – games like Snakes and Ladders, Guess Who? and Connect 4 are just a few which develop planning, problem-solving, communication and turn-taking skills

2 **Puzzles** – the silence, stillness and concentration needed to complete a puzzle all help to quieten the "downstairs" brain, while keeping the "upstairs" brain engaged. The ability to ignore distractions and persist are also developed, as well as a sense of pride once complete

3 **Traffic lights** – a good game to get children active, while paying attention, listening to and following instructions, as well as curbing impulsive behaviours

4 **Musical chairs** – this fun group game helps to boost social skills, listening, patience, conflict resolution and emotion regulation (i.e. the excitement when the child manages to sit on a chair – and their disappointment when they do not)

5 **Drawing/colouring** – develops patience, hand–eye coordination and fine motor skills. It also encourages self-expression and through inducing a similar state to meditating by minimizing agitation, regulates the brain's "panic button" – the amygdala. Think back to Maya's dysregulated moments – she reached for her journal to express her anger and hurt, by writing and drawing

6 **Musical statues** – a great way to release stress and expend energy, while developing gross motor skills, as well as the ability to listen, concentrate and follow instructions

7 **Balloon volleyball** – children build social skills while learning how to slow their movements down, to control the balloon and not let it go flying!

Things I hate!

Mum and her boyfriend Arguing!

Dad in prison!

Being picked on!

Typhoons

8 **Simon/Simone Says** – a great way to build children's SR skills, because the child must think before each action is taken, as well as listen carefully. When the child takes on the leader's role to give out instructions, this can boost self-confidence

9 **Follow my clap** – a quieter game that requires the child focus, listen carefully, remember and recall the clapping pattern, in order to repeat the actions

10 **Making and playing with playdough** – this multi-sensory activity develops hand–eye coordination and fine and gross motor skills, while helping to ease tension, release excess energy, improve focus and safely express emotions.

The experiences listed above can also be taken outdoors within the daily routine (at home or in the setting). As being outdoors in nature can exert an instantly calming effect on children during times of frustration or anger, anxiety or stress and generally help children to regain some balance. Remember – *all* children can benefit from developing their SR skills.

Connect 4

Emotion Coaching As A Co-Regulation Tool

We will now shift our attention to the evidence-based approach of Emotion Coaching (EC), which is successfully used globally to help co-regulate children's thoughts, feelings and behaviour.

EC is a relational approach (again, which means it is dependent on relationships) to supporting children's behaviour. It emphasizes the process of emotion regulation rather than behaviour modification – in other words, a focus on the emotions and desires which ultimately drive the behaviour, as opposed to focusing on the behaviour only. As Gottman and DeClaire (1997: 2) explain:

> Emotion Coaching is about helping children to understand the different emotions they experience, why they occur and how to handle them.

The emphasis on supporting children to understand their emotions and equipping them to choose different, healthier ways to respond to triggers, is fundamental to effective CR. It is what sets it apart from the more traditional behavioural strategies to supporting behaviour, which advocate a one-size-fits-all, punitive approach. Reflecting on the Stream of SR, an EC approach also means that the adult is:

✔ Aware of their own emotions

✔ Aware of the child's emotions.

EC helps to create nurturing relationships that support (or scaffold) effective stress management skills, which promote emotional and behavioural SR. It provides practitioners with a valuable tool for supporting children's behaviour while nurturing the wellbeing of both adults and children.

EC consists of three steps, as outlined by its UK founders, Dr Janet Rose and Louise Gilbert (2014: 23):

---

1 Recognizing, empathizing, validating and labelling feelings
2 Setting limits on behaviour
3 Problem-solving with the child.

Outlined below are just a few suggested statements to use as part of each of the three steps of EC. You should adapt these according to each child, their temperament, triggers and unique context.

Emotion Coaching

	Emotion Coaching step	Sample conversation prompts	Benefits to child
1	**Recognizing, empathizing, validating and labelling feelings**	"I'm sorry that happened to you, you must have felt really upset" "I would feel like this if that happened to me" "You're breathing very quickly – I can sense you feel angry" "What you're feeling is completely normal" "I understand why you feel this way"	By labelling feelings, we help to diffuse their intensity for the child. This in turn, can help them to feel calmer, quicker, which ultimately paves the way for the following two steps
2	**Setting limits on behaviour**	"It's ok to feel this way, but that behaviour isn't ok" "This isn't a safe place to be angry. Let's go somewhere safe and we can talk" "I see you're frustrated, but behaving like that is dangerous/not helpful" "We don't hurt ourselves or others – we need to follow the rules"	By setting clear limits on behaviour, we respectfully and sensitively support the child to follow rules, while acknowledging how they are feeling. Once we have set limits, we can progress to the third step (as follows)
3	**Problem-solving with the child**	"How are you feeling now?" "What does your body feel like now?" "How do you feel about the way you responded?" "Can you think of a different way to cope next time?" "I can help you to think of some different ways to cope next time" "Let's decide what you will do next time you feel like this"	When the child feels calmer and is more open to – and able to – talk, explore together what gave rise to their emotions and behaviour. You can then talk through alternative, healthier ways they could respond in the future and the benefits for them in the long-term.

EC reminds us and children that all emotions are acceptable, but not all behaviours.

It is important to understand that EC is not a one-size-fits all approach – what works with one child, might not work with another. Nor is it a "quick fix" solution. It will take time and trial and error to find out what works best with each individual child. It is also worth bearing in mind that what works with one child one day, might not be as effective the next day – so be prepared to be flexible in your approach.

Ultimately, EC works! It works to not only improve children's behaviour, but research (Gottman and DeClaire, 1997) has shown that Emotion Coached children:

- ✔ Are more emotionally stable – because they have the skills to calm themselves down when they need to
- ✔ Are more resilient – because they are more confident in handling life's ups and downs
- ✔ Achieve more academically in school – because they are able to self-regulate and are therefore ready and able to learn
- ✔ Are more popular – because they do not "flip their lid", are able to compromise and can make and maintain friendships
- ✔ Have fewer behavioural problems – because they can regulate their emotional responses and behaviour (which includes the ability to think before they act)
- ✔ Have fewer infectious illnesses – because they can regulate their fight-or-flight response, which if constantly activated, compromises immunity.

We will now turn our attention to the third approach to co-regulating dysregulated children and what this might look like.

3 The Structure of the Indoor and Outdoor Environments

Your setting and provision will make all the difference to a child's ability to self-regulate – or not. It is therefore important to hold in mind that your setting in general, needs to be SR-ready. For example, having a SR space in a setting that is otherwise cluttered and disorganized, will undermine your efforts to co-regulate children and send the wrong messages to them – and their families. You also need to ensure that your setting is well resourced to support children's SR skills, not least because these resources will further enhance the work you already do to co-regulate through your responsive relationships, modelling and the set-up of your environments. Your resources will show the children and their primary carers that you care about their mental health and that you are making the effort to prioritise this alongside academic outcomes. Most resources to support SR can be used both indoors and outdoors.

Create a Self-Regulation Space

Also known as calming corners, or zen zones, SR spaces are a quiet space – *not* a reading area, home or cosy corner and where possible, they are best designed and built *with* the children. Their purpose is to provide a quiet space away from daily activities, where the child can go to calm down – either with an adult or alone.

Once you have introduced and discussed the purpose of the SR space with children and your team, the child should always self-elect to spend some time in the SR space – it must never be forced/ordered by you. It can however, be recommended by you (or another adult), particularly as part of step 3 (problem-solving with the child) of EC.

SR spaces must be in full view of everyone, as opposed to being shut off from view. SR spaces can be provided in any type of setting – be this a home, nursery, school, outreach or family/supervised contact centre, for example.

Below are a few tips to help you when thinking about the type of SR space you want to create:

✔ The SR space must be separate to other cosy spaces, such as dens

✔ It should include a neutral-coloured rug and cushions

✔ Some soft toys for children to cuddle (cleaned regularly)

✔ A blanket

✔ Communication aids that enable a child to identify and express their feelings in-the-moment. For example, break cards. These enable a child to identify and express their feelings, while giving them the option of having a break to self-regulate before they return to the day's routine

✔ Sensory bottles (or similar resources) which could be made with the children

✔ Laminated breathing stars which staff would model for the children

✔ Family photographs

✔ Noise-cancelling headphones

✔ Squeezy objects (such as stress balls)

✔ Fidget toys

✔ Stories about feelings.

Below are some examples of indoor and outdoor SR spaces used in various educational settings and the types of resources that are often included in them.

Take a look at each of the SR spaces and think about what makes them all inviting and soothing to be in.

Self-Regulation Space 1

This SR space is proving very successful in one nursery. Look at the resources. Included in the boxes are:

✔ Laminated breathing stars – these are effective in supporting children to regulate their breathing during emotionally charged times

✔ Emotion flashcards – these are useful in supporting children to recognize and regulate their own feelings and emotions, as well as recognizing and empathizing with the emotions of others

✔ Books about emotions and significant events that can feel overwhelming (like moving home, the death of a loved one or a pet). You would buy books in line with the children's needs

✔ Stress balls – can be helpful in releasing tension and energy.

Non-intrusive, pastel colours are used, alongside soft furnishings in this SR space, to help soothe children who may have entered a state of hyper-arousal. The arch and cushions create a slightly enclosed feel, to help the child feel "contained" and physically safe.

Now look at this outdoor SR space below.

This SR space was created by children and staff in the garden of the setting.

Nature can be immediately highly effective in supporting children's ability to self-regulate. There is something instantly grounding about being out in nature – and its benefits to holistic wellbeing and behaviour are manifold. Improved attention, lower stress reactivity and elevated mood are well-documented for children and adults alike. Having a SR space outdoors can therefore be all the more useful in building children's ability to self-regulate in times of need.

Self-Regulation Space 2

Included as part of this SR space are:

✔ Durable materials used to create the space, such as artificial turf and tarpaulin

✔ Fiddle sticks

✔ Various sensory toys

✔ Rain tubes – the sound of gently falling rain can feel soothing for children and adults alike and is harmonious and relaxing

✔ (Zebra-printed) blankets for children to wrap themselves up in – this "cocooning" helps an anxious child to feel protected and secure

✔ Fresh lavender (known for its anxiety-relieving and relaxing properties), planted by the children.

Now look at the SR space on the right.

This space is loved by the younger children especially, who love to snuggle in with the large teddy bear during times of anxiety and when experiencing separation anxiety. They tend to prefer being alone in this space, with the adult close by. When they feel more regulated and are ready, they re-join the group experiences.

The SR spaces and their resources will obviously differ according to the environment you live/work in. As mentioned, getting the child/ren involved in the designing and making process will play in important part in making them feel respected, listened to, valued and helpful – all invaluable in encouraging healing from exposure to ACEs.

Self-Regulation Space 3

Discussion Prompts and Questions – Some Useful Tips

Now that we have explored some of the theory underpinning ACEs and SR, we will think about how best to support the child as you share the story together.

It is first important to think about what you aim to achieve through reading the storybook with the child – this also means taking into account their personality, their triggers, what they respond well to and what does not work so well. You also need to make the child feel physically and psychologically comfortable before sharing the story.

Below are just a few reminders:

Before settling down to read the story book together, remember to:

✔ Find somewhere comfortable to sit – somewhere away from the scheduled activities and other children. A place furnished with cushions, a blanket and soft toys for the child to hold and snuggle into would be ideal

✔ Explain in simple terms what the story is about and that it might be helpful to the child if you read and talk about it together

✔ Assure the child that he or she is safe and that you will stop reading if they want you to

✔ Explain to and reassure the child that they are not responsible for *any* of what is happening to them or in the home. Children often blame themselves for events that are completely out of their control

✔ Be patient – give the child as long as they need to talk or answer any (**non-leading**) questions without interrupting them. They might be feeling nervous or frightened

✔ Take the child's lead – if the child starts to tell you about their experiences in relation to the story while you are reading, prioritise this and let them talk.

Maya and Miss Hero Reading

Discussion Prompts and Questions

The following suggested discussion prompts and questions are designed to enable you to reflect on the events in the story with the child, with a view to supporting the child to safely express their thoughts, feelings and emotions during and after reading the story together.

The list is comprehensive but is by no means intended to be prescriptive or exhaustive – you are encouraged to amend, leave out and add to the prompts and questions, as you think is best: your knowledge of the child, their temperament, level of understanding and their unique situation will guide you.

You will note that the final question/prompt for each scene is always the same: *"What makes Maya feel happy/safe in this scene? Let's try to spot them together."* This is to enable you to highlight with the child, all the positive, protective factors in Maya's life. You could then use this as a catalyst to ask the child about all the protective factors in their life, so that they can identify the more positive elements that make them feel psychologically safe and happy.

You can also encourage the child to further express their thoughts, feelings and answers to the questions and the general discussion you have of the story together in different ways, including drawing or painting a picture, building a model from LEGO® or playdough.

Below is an outline of the main points made in each of the scenes in the story. You can use these as prompts to start a conversation with the child/ren about:

- What they think is happening in the story, in that scene

- How they think Maya is feeling – and how they might feel if they were in a similar situation to Maya.

Again, each scene prompt ends the same – that is, for you to help the child to identify what makes Maya feel happy or at least psychologically safe in that particular scene. This can then lead to a conversation which helps the child to think about any protective factors in their life – or how these can be created.

Maya in Her Bedroom

- How does Maya's face look?

- What do you think is troubling Maya?

- What do you think those butterflies and knots in Maya's tummy mean?

- If something frightens you, where in your body do you feel it? The adult could also link it to themselves, to make it feel less pressurizing: for example, "I notice that my heart beats very quickly when I'm scared of something." They could also invite the child to draw their answer

- Who does Maya speak with about her feelings?

- Do you have a pet?/Would you like to tell me about them?

- How does Harry make Maya feel?

- Why do you think Maya started to feel a slight glow inside her?

- How might Maya be feeling, hearing all the noise from the objects being thrown and smashing?

- Why do you think Maya is in her bedroom?

- Why does Maya whisper to herself *"dreams, come tonight – help make it right!"*?

- Do you have words that you like to say to yourself, to help you feel strong?/Shall we try to come up with something together?

- What makes Maya feel happy/safe in this scene? Let's try to spot them together.

Kaleidoscopic Rainforest Dreamworld

- It looks like Maya and Harry are about to go on an exciting dream adventure! What do you think might happen?

- How is Maya feeling?

- Why do you think Maya likes the dreamworld?

- Maya helps the arguing birds to solve their problem. How do you think this makes her feel?

- What makes you feel strong/confident?

- I like the sound of having *keepers*! How does this make Maya feel?

- Do you have any *keepers* – objects that remind you how special and strong you are?

- How about you start a collection of your very own *keepers*? Like Maya, you could keep them somewhere safe

- Why does Maya feel a warm glow from inside?

- What or who makes you feel warm and happy inside?

- What makes Maya feel happy/safe in this scene? Let's try to spot them together.

Breakfast

- How do you think Maya is feeling, sat at the breakfast table?

- I see Maya found the maths test at school a bit tricky, because of the arguing the night before. Could Maya have done anything to help her prepare last night? (For example, listening to music through earphones, to cut out the background noise, could be suggested)

- What makes Maya feel happy/safe in this scene? Let's try to spot them together.

Maya Talking with Her Mum about Her Dad Being in Prison

- Those butterflies and knots are back in Maya's tummy again – why do you think this is?

- Why doesn't Maya want to see her dad?

- When Maya feels angry, it's like a volcano is about to erupt inside her. What does "angry" feel like for you?

- Maya's dad is in prison. That must be very difficult for her. How might she be feeling?

- What could help her when she feels sad about this?

- What makes Maya feel happy/safe in this scene? Let's try to spot them together.

Ocean Dreamworld

- The pretty patterns of the ripples in the water make Maya feel calm. What helps you to feel calm?

- Well done to Harry for showing Maya to do deep breathing to help her calm down! Do you ever do deep breathing to help calm you down?

- Shall we give it a go now? (The suggestions for fun breathing exercises in this guide could be used here)

- Maya and Harry certainly work well as a team to solve problems! Who helps you to work through any problems you might have?

- What makes Maya feel happy/safe in this scene? Let's try to spot them together.

Maya Visiting Her Dad in Prison

- How do you think Maya feels about not being able to see her dad whenever she likes?

- What could Maya and her mum do to help Maya feel less scared about visiting her dad in prison?

- Maya's feeling nervous, waiting to see her dad. I would be too. How might you feel?

- What could Maya bring to her next visit to comfort her while she waits to see her dad?

- What could Maya and her mum do after the visit?

- What do you think it would be like to have a parent in prison?

- What makes Maya feel happy/safe in this scene? Let's try to spot them together.

At School/Hannah Picking on Maya

- Who do you like to play with at school?

- What's your best part of the school day? (Here, the adult could mention their favourite aspect of school, as a child)

- It's good that Maya has someone she can speak with at school about her dad. Who do you like to speak with if something is worrying you?

- How does Maya look in that picture?

- What makes you feel angry?

- I can understand Maya feeling angry at Hannah – that was a mean thing to say. What would you have done, if you were Maya?

- What makes Maya feel happy/safe in this scene? Let's try to spot them together.

Maya Writing in Her Journal in Her Bedroom

- Things are difficult for Maya, especially at the moment. I see she likes to draw about how she is feeling. That's a good idea. Do you ever draw pictures when you're feeling upset? (The adult could extend the dialogue in response to the child's answers)

- Maya's mum is very understanding. Who do you like to speak with at home, if something is worrying you?

- Maya still seems angry and upset. What else could she do to try to feel a bit better about what happened at school?

- Why do you think Maya's heart started to beat faster and her breathing became quicker?

- Does this ever happen to you? When do you notice it happening?

- Look at Maya in this picture, as she's practising some deep breathing. How does she look in the picture? Remember the breathing exercises we spoke about earlier? You might like to try them at home, to help you feel calm. If you do, please let me know how it goes!

- What makes Maya feel happy/safe in this scene? Let's try to spot them together.

Circus Dreamworld

- Poor Harry – now he's being picked on. What would you do to help him?

- Maya did well to defend Harry, but now she's upset thinking about her dad in prison. What could she do the next time she thinks about her dad and feels upset?

- I wonder how Maya will use that juggling ball? What do you think?

- What makes Maya feel happy/safe in this scene? Let's try to spot them together.

Meeting with Miss Hero and Hannah

- Maya sometimes finds it difficult to say how she feels. She likes to draw how she feels too. How do you most like to show how you're feeling? (The adult can give their own examples as prompts too)

- How do you think Maya felt about going into the meeting? I think she was very brave. When have you felt brave?

- Well done to Hannah – she probably felt uneasy in that meeting. What would you have said to Hannah in that meeting?

- I like Maya's idea for using the juggling ball! I think the idea of collecting *keepers* as a reminder of all the good things is a great idea. Perhaps you could bring in any of your own *keepers* for us to look at together, next time I see you?

- What makes Maya feel happy/safe in this scene? Let's try to spot them together.

Maya Writing in Her Journal Before Bedtime

- Maya's idea to make a list of all the good things in her life is so important. What do you think?

- Shall we write a list of all the good things in your life? Or, if you prefer, you could do this at home and show me the next time I see you. You choose!

- I really like Maya's mantra – that sentence she says to remind her that she *is* strong. How about we think of a positive mantra for you? What do you think? It might help to make *you* feel strong, when you need it

- What makes Maya feel happy/safe in this scene? Let's try to spot them together.

What to Do If a Child Makes an In-the-Moment Disclosure

Before sharing the storybook with the child, it is important to consider the possibility of them disclosing their experience of abuse and/or neglect to you. This is so that you are very clear about the remit and responsibility of *your* role specifically.

While reading the storybook with the child, they might start to tell you about their own experiences – and your responses to their in-the-moment disclosure are critical, both with regard to the child's emotional wellbeing and the integrity of the case, should there already be one underway. Where a case is already open, all relevant agencies and professionals should be working together, in line with agreed plans and shared agreements. This means that information sharing procedures and any work done with the child must not be done in isolation. While we want to facilitate open discussion, this must be part of a wider response to the child's needs and may require collaboration with specialist statutory services such as social services or the police.

Although the purpose of the storybook is not to instigate a disclosure, it might be an inevitable outcome of reading the storybook together. It is therefore important that you feel as confident and competent as possible (both emotionally and professionally) when responding to a child's in-the-moment disclosure. According to Baker et al., (2019: 4) a disclosure is:

> The process of a child starting to share their experiences with others. This process can start before the child is ready to put their thoughts and feelings in order. The process can be verbal and/or non-verbal and can take place over a long period of time – it is a journey, not one act or action.

During an in-the-moment disclosure, you may instinctively feel shocked, panicked, upset or even triggered yourself. The following suggestions could help you to respond as appropriately and sensitively as possible:

✔ Respond calmly – do not express shock or disgust at anything the child tells you, as this could distress or further distress them

DOI: 10.4324/b23180-15

✔ Do not express any opinions about the alleged abuser

✔ Listen carefully and attentively

✔ Take the child seriously

✔ Reassure the child that they have taken the right action in talking to you

✔ **Do not, under any circumstances, promise to keep anything secret**

✔ Check back with the child that what you have heard is correct and understood

✔ Ask questions for clarification only – **do not ask any leading questions**

✔ Ensure that the child understands that you must tell someone who can help

✔ Make a written record of what the child has told you as soon as possible, in as much detail as possible

✔ Treat the information confidentially

✔ Inform your setting's DSL without delay and report the disclosure made to you

✔ Continue to support the child in line with the setting's safeguarding and child protection procedures.

Levels of Need

Depending on the nature of a disclosure, i.e. what the child is communicating with the adult, an appropriate response will involve making professional judgements and taking subsequent actions. The needs of the child may already be determined through processes such as early help or a child in need (CIN) assessment. A disclosure has the potential to highlight the following, in terms of levels of need for a child:

- Information previously unknown, suggesting a low-level concern and that the child should be best supported though early help assessment and intervention

- Changes in a situation (level of need) – identifying that there is an increased level of risk and therefore the needs of the child have escalated (often from early help level to CIN or child protection (CP) plan)

- The information suggests that the child is at risk of Significant Harm and therefore their needs require statutory services to be informed to intervene and protect them.

The disclosure might also offer new information concerning a child who is undergoing a CIN assessment, which will therefore be considered as relevant to the overall assessment. Additionally, a child in care who discloses may have the information of their disclosure used in court as evidence for court proceedings. To reiterate, following organisational safeguarding and CP policies and procedures, including the importance of recording and record-keeping, is of paramount importance.

Significant Harm

If a child's disclosure leads you to conclude that the threshold of Significant Harm is met, then a referral to social services should be considered by the setting's DSL. If in doubt, your setting's policies and procedures should be sufficient to guide you in taking the appropriate action(s) to help support and safeguard the child.

Although Significant Harm has no steadfast definition, under Section 31(9) of the Children Act 1989, as amended by the Adoption and Children Act 2002:

- Harm means ill-treatment or impairment of health or development including for example impairment suffered from seeing or hearing the ill-treatment of another* (...)

- Ill-treatment includes sexual abuse and forms of ill-treatment which are not physical.

*The Adoption and Children Act 2002 broadens the definition of Significant Harm to include the emotional harm suffered by those children who witness domestic violence or are aware of domestic violence within their home environment.

There are no absolute criteria on which to rely when judging what constitutes Significant Harm. Consideration of the severity of ill-treatment may include:

- The degree and extent of physical harm;

- The duration and frequency of abuse or neglect;

- The extent of premeditation;

- The degree of threats and coercion;

- Evidence of sadism, and bizarre or unusual elements in child sexual abuse (...).

Sometimes, a single traumatic event may constitute Significant Harm. In other circumstances Significant Harm is caused by the cumulative effect of significant events, both acute and long-standing, or the damaging impact of neglect which interrupt and change or damage the child's physical and psychological development.

(Voice of the Child, 2022)

In order to decide what constitutes Significant Harm, you will liaise with a range of professionals involved with the child, who, together, must take the following factors into consideration:

- The family context, including the family's strengths and supports

- The child's development within the context of the family and within the context of the wider social and cultural environment

- Any special needs, such as a medical condition, communication difficulty or disability that may affect the child's development and care within the family

- The nature of harm in terms of the ill-treatment or failure to provide adequate care

- The impact on the child's health and development

- The adequacy of parental care.

(Voice of the Child, 2022)

Summary and Final Thoughts

The purpose of this adult guide was to build understanding around ACEs and their impact on children's holistic wellbeing, behaviour and ability to learn. Children who have been exposed to ACEs are too frequently met with judgement, labelled and left unsupported. This is particularly true of the one-size-fits-all education system, which generally relies on outmoded and harmful approaches to controlling and stamping out behaviours deemed "challenging", as opposed to equipping teachers and other school staff to work in ways that are more relational.

Critiques of the ACEs framework were also introduced, to remind us that ACEs are *not* destiny – and that with the support of responsive, nurturing adults and other protective factors, children exposed to ACEs can achieve whatever they wish to. Aligned to this, key concepts were also included, such as SR and the critical role of CR in nurturing its development. On which note:

Reflect on whether you're an effective stress detective – and with this in mind:

Always Be Curious!

Useful Resources

The following list includes a range of resources that might be helpful to the children and families you work with. It is important to check through the resources before recommending them, to ensure their suitability. Even if you find that they are not directly relevant, it is often worthwhile checking the bibliography and list of resources on their respective websites, as these often contain sound general advice and guidance, as well as some other subject-specific resources.

- **Barnardo's** – this charity helps children with a parent in prison. They run training services for professionals, as well as services in the community and in prisons to help maintain contact and support family relationships:
barnardos.org.uk

- **Beacon House** – contains a diverse range of resources (and services) for families and practitioners alike to use, to better understand child and family mental health and the importance of secure attachments in nurturing SR and prosocial behaviour:
https://beaconhouse.org.uk/

- **Bright Sky App** – this is a safe and easy to use app (available via Apple and Google Store) and website, providing practical support and information on how to respond to domestic abuse. It is for anyone experiencing domestic abuse, or who is worried about someone else:
https://www.hestia.org/brightsky

- **Childline** – a counselling service for children and young people up to their 19th birthday in the UK, provided by the NSPCC:
08001111 (freephone)

- **Keep Your Cool Toolbox** – also available as a free app (on Android phones), this award-winning resource provides quick and effective ways to help children and young people to better manage their emotions:
https://keepyourcooltoolbox.com/

- **NICCO (the National Information Centre on Children of Offenders)** – an information hub that provides a support service for all professionals who come into contact with the children and families of offenders. It also provides materials for academics and those responsible for strategic development and commissioning of family services:
https://www.nicco.org.uk/

- **NSPCC (National Society for the Prevention of Cruelty to Children)** – this leading children's charity in the UK provides therapeutic services to help children move on from abuse, as well as supporting parents and families in caring for their children. Their website is full of accessible information for children, families and practitioners alike:
  nspcc.org.uk

- **Place2Be** – this children's mental health charity offers a wide range of services to children, families and staff in schools, to support children's mental health:
  http://www.place2be.org.uk

- **Prisoners' Families' Helpline** – this helpline offers support and information for prisoners, people with convictions, defendants and their families:
  0808 808 203 (freephone)

- **Refuge National Domestic Abuse Website and Helpline** – the website is packed full of resources and instant support for individuals experiencing domestic abuse, as well as those who know someone experiencing domestic abuse. Support is also available on the website in the form of a discreet live online chat, from Monday to Friday, between 3pm and 10pm, for those who find it difficult to speak on the phone. Refuge also has a British Sign Language interpreter service which is available from Monday to Friday, between 10am to 6pm:
  https://refuge.org.uk
  National Domestic Abuse Helpline 0808 2000 247 (freephone)

- **Samaritans** – Samaritans are available to listen to children (and adults) about their problems 24 hours a day, 365 days a year:
  116 123 (freephone)

- **YoungMinds** – this charity provides young people with tools to look after their mental health. Their website is full of advice and information for young people and parents, as well as practitioners who work with children and young adults:
  youngminds.org.uk

Bibliography

Allnock, D. and Miller, P. (2013). *No One Noticed, No One Heard: A Study of Disclosures of Childhood Abuse*. London: NSPCC.

Baker, H., Miller, P., Starr, E., Witcombe-Hayes, S. and Gwilym, C. (2019). *Let Children Know You're Listening: The Importance of an Adult's Interpersonal Skills in Helping to Improve the Child's Experiences of Disclosure*. London: NSPCC.

Bellis, M. A., Hughes, K., Leckenby, N., Perkins, C. and Lowey, H. (2014). National household survey of adverse childhood experiences and their relationship with resilience to health-harming behaviours in England. *BMC Medicine*, 12(72): 1–10.

Brown, D. W., Anda, R. F., Tiemeier, H., Felitti, V. J., Edwards, V. J., Croft, J. B. and Giles, W. H. (2009). Adverse childhood experiences and the risk of premature mortality. *Am J Prev Med*, 37(5): 389–396.

Callaghan, J. E., Alexander, J. H., Sixsmith, J. and Fellin, L. C. (2015). Beyond "witnessing": Children's experiences of coercive control in domestic violence and abuse. *Journal of Interpersonal Violence*, 33 (10): 1551–1581.

Conkbayir, M. (2023). *The Neuroscience of the Developing Child. Self-Regulation for Wellbeing and a Sustainable Future*. London: Routledge.

Felitti, V. J., Anda, R. F., Nordenberg, D., Williamson, D. F., Spitz, A. M., Edwards, V., Koss, M. P. and Marks, J. S. (1998). Relationship of childhood abuse and household dysfunction to many of the leading causes of death in adults. The Adverse Childhood Experiences (ACE) Study. *American Journal of Preventive Medicine*, 14: 245–258.

Gottman, J. M. and DeClaire, J. (1997). *Raising an Emotionally Intelligent Child: The Heart of Parenting*. New York: Simon & Schuster.

Heckman, J. J. and Karapakula, G. (2019). *Intergenerational and Intragenerational Externalities of the Perry Preschool Project* (May). NBER Working Paper No. w25889, Available at SSRN: https://ssrn.com/abstract=3399272

Hughes, K., Bellis, M. A., Hardcastle, K. A., Sethi, D., Butchart, A., Mikton, C., Jones, L. and Dunne, M. P. (2017). The effect of multiple adverse childhood experiences on health: A systematic review and meta-analysis. *Lancet Public Health*, 2: 356–366.

Kelly-Irving, M. and Delpierre, C. (2019). A critique of the adverse childhood experiences framework in epidemiology and public health: Uses and misuses. *Social Policy and Society*, 18(3): 445–456.

Kohn, A. (2018). *Punished By Rewards: Twenty-Fifth Anniversary Edition: The Trouble with Gold Stars, Incentive Plans, A's, Praise, and Other Bribes*. San Francisco: HarperOne.

Rosanbalm, K. D. and Murray, D. W. (2017). Caregiver Co-regulation Across Development: A Practice Brief. OPRE Brief #2017–80. Washington, DC: Office of Planning, Research, and Evaluation, Administration for Children and Families, US. Department of Health and Human Services.

Seeman, T., Epel, E., Gruenewald, T., Karlamangla, A. and McEwen, B. S. (2010). Socio-economic differentials in peripheral biology: Cumulative allostatic load. *Ann N Y Acad Sci*, 1186(1): 223–239.

Shanker, S. (2020). *Reframed*. Toronto, Buffalo and London: University of Toronto Press.

Siegel, D. and Bryson, T. (2012). *The Whole Brain Child: 12 Revolutionary Strategies to Nurture Your Child's Developing Mind*. London: Robinson.

Taylor-Robinson, D. C., Straatmann, V. S. and Whitehead, M. (2018). Adverse childhood experiences or adverse childhood socioeconomic conditions? *The Lancet Public Health*, 3(6): 61–63.

Websites

The Adoption and Children Act 2002. Legislation.gov.uk https://www.legislation.gov.uk/ukpga/2002/38/contents (accessed 4th September 2022)

barnardos.org.uk (accessed 4th September 2022)

https://beaconhouse.org.uk/ (accessed 4th September 2022)

Cambridge Dictionary (2022). Tantrum. Cambridge: Cambridge University Press. (Online) https://dictionary.cambridge.org/dictionary/english/tantrum (accessed 4th September 2022)

Centers for Disease Control and Prevention (2020). https://www.cdc.gov/violenceprevention/aces/about.html?CDC_AA_refVal=https%3A%2F%2Fwww.cdc.gov%2Fviolence prevention%2Facestudy%2Fabout.html (accessed 4th September 2022)

Children Act 1989. https://www.legislation.gov.uk/ukpga/1989/41/contents (accessed 4th September 2022)

https://keepyourcooltoolbox.com/ (accessed 4th September 2022)

https://www.nicco.org.uk/ (accessed 4th September 2022)

NSPCC (2022). https://learning.nspcc.org.uk/child-protection-system/child-protection-definitions (accessed 4th September 2022)

Oxford Learner's Dictionary (2022). Tantrum. Oxford: Oxford University Press. (Online) https://www.oxfordlearnersdictionaries.com/definition/english/tantrum?q=TANTRUM (accessed 4th September 2022)

http://www.place2be.org.uk (accessed 4th September 2022)

Santucci, G. (2021). https://www.seattleschild.com/family-review-of-the-issaquah-salmon-hatchery-this-was-really-great/ (accessed 4th September 2022)

Voice of the Child (2022). https://www.voiceofthechild.org.uk/kb/recognition-significant-harm/ (accessed 4th September 2022)

youngminds.org.uk (accessed 4th September 2022)

Wikipedia (2022). Tantrum. https://en.wikipedia.org/wiki/Tantrum (accessed 4th September 2022)

Index

Page numbers in **bold** refer to illustrations